BARGAINING ESSENTIALS

How to Successfully Bargain from Survey to Settlement and Maximize Your Wins

Doc Dengenis

Bargaining Training and Strategy Consultant

Third Printing

DEDICATION

This book is dedicated to my mother, Rosamond Dengenis, and my brothers, Frank Joseph Dengenis, Jr., and Michael Dengenis, all deceased. In addition, it is for my beloved children Petra Dengenis Roberts, Champ, Brig Dengenis and my new grandson, Burton Roberts.

This book is also for James T. Hart, an outstanding Linfield College economics professor, who inspired my lifelong interest in labor relations.

Finally, it is for my Uncle Carmine DeVito, longtime business agent for the Bricklayers, Masons, and Plasterers Union Local 1 in the Greater Hartford area in Connecticut, who was a role model for the Dengenis boys.

ACKNOWLEDGMENTS

Brig Dengenis provided computer expertise and advice pertinent to the successful completion of *Bargaining Essentials.* Bob Ferguson and Danny Jacobson were valuable sources for my first venture in writing a book. Kristen Hall-Geisler provided valuable copy edit services.

LIFE

Life is a rollercoaster full of appointments and disappointments. I have told my children on numerous occasions to celebrate their appointments and move on quickly from their disappointments. I celebrate the successful completion and publishing of *Bargaining Essentials.*

TABLE OF CONTENTS

BARGAINING ESSENTIALS

PREFACE

Bargaining Essentials explains the important foundations of the bargaining process. This is a valuable resource document for all bargainers, regardless of skill level or experience. Readers will have the opportunity to develop and practice bargaining skills, techniques, tactics, and strategies in a wide variety of exercises and a final bargaining simulation. The emphasis is on developing and tracking a bargaining blueprint, using sufficient consensus as a decision making model, writing proposals and counterproposals, executing tentative agreements, formulating caucus concepts, questioning strategies, verbal skills, performing single issue bargaining and package bargaining, doing package analysis, stair stepping proposals, devising "Supposals", and learning advanced negotiation skills and strategies. Also included are templates for minutes and bargaining newsletters. This "how and when" resource book is a result of my thirty years of successful bargaining, organizing, and training experiences. Strategies to get around roadblocks at the table are explored in depth so the reader has new tools to deal with local bargaining problems.

BARGAINING TEAM BUILDING EXERCISE

The purpose of this exercise is to get full disclosure from all team members and prevent last minute hidden agendas that could block final closure when settling a contract.

1. My name is _____ and I have worked at _____ for the last _____ years.

1. My main responsibility at work is

_____.

2. The sum total of my bargaining experience is

_____

_____.

4. I am on this bargaining team because

_____

_____.

5. I will be satisfied at the conclusion of bargaining if the team is successful in accomplishing

_____

_____

_____.

DEFINITION OF BARGAINING

Bargaining is a process designed to manage conflict and produce a written document specifying the wages, hours, and conditions of employment mutually agreed upon by the Parties.

The nature of bargaining means there will be some conflict, stress, pressure, tension and disagreement inherent in the process, both at the table and in your caucus. It is unavoidable. People who are unable to cope with these pressures should not be on a bargaining team.

The main objective of the bargain is to meet our member's needs.

CONFLICT

1. There are natural conflicts inherent in employee employer bargaining.

2. Natural conflicts will occur whether a traditional or collaborative bargaining relationship exists.

3. The key is how to manage these conflicts.

4. The ability to survive and thrive in managing conflict both at the table and in caucuses is essential in order to have a successful bargaining team.

THE THREE MOST IMPORTANT COMPONENTS
OF A SUCCESSFUL BARGAIN

1.   Preparation

2. Preparation

3. PREPARATION

Team preparation is just as important as what happens at the table.

POWER DEFINED

A bargaining relationship is based upon power, both real and perceived. If you do not have power when you go to the table, you will not find it there. A team can even lose power at the table.

1. If there is a longstanding, clear, and unbroken past practice, do not introduce any issue at the table unless the team is ready to go to the mat to preserve it.
2. If a team takes an issue to the table and does not succeed in bargaining it into the contract, then it is lost.

THE DIFFERENCE BETWEEN "POWER" ORGANIZING AND "ACTIVITY" ORGANIZING

"Activity" organizing works when a settlement is close. A strong demonstration of support, through an activity or a short series of organized activities, is essential in order to generate sufficient pressure to finalize an agreement.

"Power" organizing works when there is a wide gap in the issues and a settlement is not imminent. A comprehensive organizing plan is developed with a series of escalating activities, and the members are prepared to withhold services as a last resort. It is not necessary to apologize for taking this approach; at times it is necessary in order to achieve a fair settlement.

THE ASSOCIATION'S POWER SOURCE

Our power base is with our members.

The ability and willingness of the organization to organize its members to collective action is our primary power source.

Effective organizations have the ability to pull together for collective action during a crisis.

The Association bargaining team has power and does not have to apologize for utilizing it responsibly.

The Association normally has much more power than the bargaining team perceives.

Organizing is the key.

THE DIFFERENCE BETWEEN "POWER" BARGAINING AND "RATIONAL" BARGAINING

1. "Rational" bargaining is when the Association goes to the table and verbalizes its positions without having organized member support for the team and the issues. In short, there is little or no member support or activity.

2. "Power" bargaining is coming from a position of maximum support from the members for the team and issues accompanied by an organizing plan with visible signs of support and solidarity. The members receive a bargaining report after every session.

MAJOR BARGAINING PITFALLS TO AVOID

1. Falling into Management's artificial timeline trap. It is essential to work off the Association time line.

2. Compromising for the sole purpose of reducing the gap between the parties.

3. Not preparing your team on all the issues on the table.

4. Talking too much! Highly skilled, experienced bargainers are effective sensors. There is a reason why we have two ears and one mouth.

MAJOR POWER MISTAKES

1. Do not underestimate your own power, as long as members are supportive of the team and the issues.

2. Do not be intimidated by lawyers since only a few issues in a contract relate to the law and attorneys know very little about daily working conditions. In general, attorneys do not understand and have a difficult time dealing with organizing.

3. Do not be swayed by statistics, precedents, principles, rules, regulations, or other data unless it is in the best interests of the members.

4. Management will suffer big losses, financial and otherwise, in the event of a job action or work stoppage.

BARGAINING TEAM DECISION MAKING IN CAUCUS

Do not use in front of the other team

The calling for the thumbs is always done in caucus and never in front of Management.

Background:

1. All team members must agree to a decision making process before the start of bargaining preparation.

2. Do not change the decision making process when faced with a difficult decision.

3. Teams need to know when their members are "in agreement" as to how to proceed or on accepting or rejecting a management offer.

The following are three models for making decisions:

1. Consensus – All team members agree on a decision.

2. Sufficient Consensus – A meeting of the minds where every member of the team is given the opportunity to participate in the discussion and decision. Not everyone may like the decision, but everyone is willing to live with it and will not undermine or sabotage the decision.

   The team has the power to declare "sufficient consensus" in the event that members continue to be blockers by saying "no" while not offering viable options or alternatives within a reasonable, specified time frame.

3. Majority Rule – Half plus one decides. This facilitates the easiest decision-making. However, it can also put team unity to the test. This is a way to make a final decision in order to meet an absolute deadline in case a team cannot reach sufficient consensus.

EFFICIENT WAY TO ACHIEVE SUFFICIENT CONSENSUS—AND SAVE TIME AND ENERGY

Thumb System:

1. Up is yes.

2. Down is no.

3. Sideways meets minimum requirement.

4. The team should continue discussion and/or proceed with extreme caution in the event more than one person has voted sideways.

5. A "down thumb" requires the "down" member(s) to offer viable alternatives within a reasonable time frame so it is not a veto.

**Each team member votes on every decision, every time –
NO EXCEPTIONS.**

The Consensus Captain

1. Team selects a member to insure everyone votes on every issue every time.

2. The captain "calls for the thumbs" when the discussion is finished.

3. Normally, the consensus captain is not the spokesperson.

SUFFICIENT CONSENSUS EXERCISE: PRIORITIZING CONTRACT ISSUES

You are a member of a bargaining team. Several issues have been raised by members as being desirable in a new contract, listed below. There are four issues. You are to consider those issues and rate them high (1), medium (2), or low (3), in terms of importance, using sufficient consensus as the decision making model.

First, decide on the way you are going to reach sufficient consensus.

_____ Five days Association leave

_____ Salary/wage schedule improvement

_____ $500 training reimbursement for all employees

_____ IRS mileage rate

14

THE TEN COMMANDMENTS OF BARGAINING SURVEYS

1. Surveys should be done before bargaining starts.

2. Sell issues to members during and at the end of the bargain.

3. Surveys should be limited to one page, front and back.

4. Survey items should be sorted using high, medium, and low priority, or some similar scheme.

5. In a mature bargaining relationship where a contract has been in existence for a long time, only issues of some recorded importance in a survey should be on the table.

6. Surveys should not impact organizational issues like association leave and union security clauses essential for the efficient operation of the organization.

7. In general, surveys should validate the business of the bargaining team.

8. Electronic surveys expedite the information gathering process.

9. A very simple paper survey could be "other than salary/wages, and health benefits, identify the key issues for the bargain."

10. A non-paper survey can be conducted by having building and/or regional meetings to hear and scribe member's needs, concerns, and interests.

ROLES OF BARGAINING TEAM MEMBERS

On a good bargaining team, just as on any other team, each member should have a distinct role to play. The following is an example of the "line-up" for a bargaining team:

Chief Negotiator

1. Team spokesperson.
2. May delegate others to speak on specific topics.
3. Calls caucuses (other team members may suggest a caucus).
4. Calls team meetings.
5. Chief strategist.
6. In charge of team preparation for bargaining.
7. Is responsible to Association President and Executive Board.

Assistant Negotiator

1. Chief negotiator's assistant.
2. Keeps paperwork organized and ready for chief negotiator to use at right time.
3. Receives notes from team members (such as suggestions for a caucus) and passes them on at appropriate time.

Recorder

1. Takes notes on all bargaining sessions.
2. Keeps team's official bargaining record.
3. Must be a knowledgeable and effective listener and an accurate reporter.
4. Recorder's official record will become important for determining intent of language in resolving future grievances.
5. It is best to record with a computer.

Sensor/Observer

1. Extension of chief negotiator's eyes and ears.
2. Observes body language and other non-verbal behavior of other team.
3. Reports observations to chief negotiator.
4. Takes notes on anything the other team says that might be useful in reporting to members or public.
5. Listens for signs and/or signals from other team.

THE EARLY BARGAINING SESSIONS*

1. The bargaining team enters (and leaves) the room together.

2. Introduction of team members (first session).

3. Each team is responsible for its own record keeping.

4. Any ground rules (usually limited to time, place, date and future meetings) should be discussed.

5. The moving Party offers and explains a series of proposals. Normally both Parties have proposals.

6. The other team usually reads the proposals and asks a series of questions about the issues.

7. Next, one team asks for a caucus to discuss the proposals, and in due course returns to the bargaining table with written responses or counterproposals.

8. One team explains their counterproposals while the other team reviews them and asks relevant questions.

9. One team usually caucuses to prepare counterproposals to respond to the proposals.

10. This process continues until there is a signed, written Tentative Agreement that is mutually agreed upon between the Parties pending final ratification.

> ***Ascertain that each Party has the authority to bargain and reach Tentative Agreement immediately after the introductions and prior to the first item on the business agenda.**

WAYS TO SAY NO

1. "No, No, No!"

2. "No! This team will not recommend this to our members."

3. "No!" Resubmit your previous proposal or package.

4. "No! Our position remains firm on this issue, and we have no intention of moving unless you give us a close to settled or settlement package, or new information that causes us to change the issues in our package."

5. "No! This is a strike issue that needs to be satisfactorily resolved to meet our member's needs before a settlement is finalized."

6. "No!" Caucus and counter with an unacceptable alternative in order to keep both unacceptable proposals in juxtaposition for leverage purposes.

7. "No! Our leaders and members will never accept or ratify your proposal or package."

8. "No! We reject your last package proposal, since it is not even remotely close to the bargaining settlement guidelines unanimously supported by our members."

NO LANGUAGE IS BETTER THAN BAD LANGUAGE

1. "No" is a legitimate counterproposal.

2. Normally the "No" response is accompanied by the reason or reasons for saying "No."

3. It is all right to say "No." There is no need to apologize or feel bad about using "No" as a counter proposal.

4. Using a strong "No" is sometimes important when sending a message to Management about the relative importance of an issue or package.

5. Be prepared for Management to say "No" several times.

6. Utilize discovery questions for revealing real or underlying reasons for saying "No."

7. Do not counter your own proposals because Management continues to say "No."

8. Never agree to bad proposal only because it is an opportunity get starter language in the contract that can be changed the next bargain if it does not work.

ONE WAY TO SAY NO IN BARGAINING

Utilizing the "Dead Space Strategy"

NO RESPONSE

"NO" is the single most powerful word or response in bargaining.

There is also power in <u>SILENCE.</u>

BACKGROUND ON BARGAINING EXERCISE

The Association and Management have been negotiating for several weeks on a wide variety of issues. Management has introduced an alcohol testing policy in the event that there is "reasonable and justifiable" suspicion that an employee has an alcohol problem negatively impacting daily work performance .

The Management negotiator continues from time to time to introduce and engage in a long dialogue about this issue. She states that this is a high priority for the Board and has a great deal of community support because of recent press about an intoxicated employee at work in a similar industry from a nearby town.

The current contract is silent on the matter, and there is no precedent for this issue in other area or local bargaining agreements.

The Board chairperson is on the State Board Association and wants to blaze a trail for the State Association.

Instructions

1. Develop a written association strategy on the next page.

2. Prepare an association counterproposal with a written opening statement to include appropriate rationale with five reasons to be articulated at the bargaining table.

BARGAINING EXERCISE GUIDE SHEET

Association Strategy:

Opening Statement:

Counterproposal:

GROUND RULES

Management sometimes attempts to seize control of the bargaining process by introducing restrictive ground rules to govern the bargaining process. These restrictive ground rules described below should be avoided.

Restrictive Ground Rules

1. Prohibiting press releases, or allowing only joint press releases.

2. Restricting or prohibiting use of outside staff and/or consultants.

3. Restricting internal communication to members.

4. Establishing short time frames for sessions.

5. Allowing sessions to be tape recorded and/or videotaped.

The best rule to follow is to have no rules, except to agree on a time, place, and date for each meeting.

WHEN TO CAUCUS

The when and why to call a caucus are critical for a team in reaching agreement on a single item or finalizing a settlement package on a new contract. If you are unsure about an issue or there's a surprise development, call a team caucus to discuss the situation and devise a strategy.

Reasons to Caucus:

1. When disorganized.

2. To review information, strategies, tactics, counterproposals, and other creative alternatives.

3. To consult staff experts and/or consultants to clarify management rules, regulations, policies, or laws.

4. To develop new arguments, questions, or answers, or to present new evidence or testimonials.

5. To get a divided team going in the same direction.

6. To review the association blueprint.

7. When the team is too tired and not focused enough to be efficient and productive.

8. To get an Association legal opinion when presented with a bad Management legal opinion.

9. If a development does not feel right, caucus and reevaluate the process and/or the product, because it is probably not right.

JUSTIFICATIONS FOR PROPOSALS

1. Time is money.
   a. Employee time is ours to give and not Management's to demand.
   b. Management requires time. Management pays for time.

2. Problem solving.
   a. Problems must be corrected.
   b. Future problems can be prevented.

3. Equity with other local or area bargaining units.

4. Comparability with other local or area contracts.

5. Authentic participation, with a significant voice in decisions affecting daily working conditions.

6. Beneficial to employees and the employer.

7. Promote positive employee/employer relationships.

8. Members want and need it to be successful in their daily work endeavors.

BLUEPRINT FOR WRITING MEMORANDA OF AGREEMENT

SUBSTANTIVE

1. Start with Statement/Declaration of Intent, if appropriate.

2. State clearly that either this Memorandum of Agreement (MOA) is an Addendum of the Collective Bargaining Agreement or is included in the Collective Bargaining Agreement.

3. Use clear and concise language.

4. Ensure it is enforceable under contract, with the Association having the option to proceed directly to arbitration absent resolution at Step 1.

IF APPLICABLE AND/OR APPROPRIATE

5. Clearly state that the MOA does not set precedent or create any expectations for future bargaining.

6. Make sure contract will be automatically restored to previous contract standards and/or levels at expiration of MOA.

TECHNICAL/ADMINISTRATIVE

7. Dated with effective dates.

8. Duration/Expiration Date.

9. Signed by Signatory Parties.

10. Sufficient copies so each Signatory Party keeps an original signed copy.

MEMORANDUM OF AGREEMENT SAMPLE

MEMORANDUM OF AGREEMENT
BETWEEN
COMMUNITY COLLEGE
AND THE
COLLEGE FACULTY ASSOCIATION

The following Memorandum of Agreement between the Faculty Association and the College Board will become part of the Collective Bargaining Agreement dated September 1, 2009 – August 31, 2010.

Because of the severe budgetary crisis facing the College in 2009-2010, the Signatory Parties agree to find ways to strive for quality education by maintaining the continuity of instruction.

Position

This agreement is for the position of (department title) instructor vacated by (describe circumstances how this position was vacated) by (vacated instructor's name).

Background

Contract Language Reference

Article 23, C 1 and C 4 of the bargaining agreement reads:

C.   *Procedural Conditions*

> *1.In the implementation of a reduction in staff, no faculty member shall be laid off as long as part-time instruction equivalent to one FTE instructor exists and the full-time instructor is qualified to teach each of the courses and the faculty member is able and willing to teach the combination of courses at the days and times that the courses have been scheduled, if the schedule is fixed, or at the days and times that the courses reasonably can be scheduled, if the schedule is not yet fixed.*

> *4.When reduction in staff is accomplished through attrition instead of layoff, the College shall not be obligated to fill the vacant position provided, however, that fifty percent (50%) or greater equivalent part-time instruction is not substituted for the full-time vacant position.*

This memorandum of agreement (MOA) sets out the following:

1.   (A) For the benefit of the students, the continuity of instruction and at the discretion of the full-time faculty in the affected department, part-time instructor(s) will fill this vacated position with a course load of up to 45 ILC'S in 02-03. At the discretion to the full-time faculty, the assignment includes up to eight (8) paid office hours pro-rated with the term load, paid participation in division and department meetings, paid curriculum development as required, and paid participation on college-wide committees.

   (B) Individual Department request (if needed).

2. This vacated position will be advertised in the usual and customary manner as a tenure-track position no later than February 2009.

3. This MOA is grievable under the terms of Article 18 of the Collective Bargaining Agreement and the Association has the option of proceeding directly to arbitration after Step 1.

4. This MOA will be for one year in duration and will expire/sunset on June 30, 2010.

5. All terms and conditions of the collective bargaining agreement will automatically be restored to the 2008-2009 contractual levels and standards as of June 30, 2006.

6. This MOA does not set a precedent for any future bargaining, in particular Article 1, Section B, 2 and Article 23, Section C of the Agreement.

For the Faculty Association   For the College

_____   _____
Association President   College President

Dated: _____   Dated: _____

MEMORANDUM OF AGREEMENT TEAM EXERCISE

1.   Crosscheck the blueprint for writing a Memorandum of Agreement against the example MOA.

2.   Write an X or dot in each appropriate box if it is designated in the Memorandum of Agreement.

BARGAINING NEWSLETTER TEMPLATE

Location: _____ Date: _____

Starting Time: _____ Ending Time: _____

Association Team Present: _____

_____

_____

Management Team Present: _____

_____

_____

Progress: _____

_____

_____

_____

_____

_____

_____

Problems: _____

_____

_____

_____

_____

_____

Quotes: _____

_____

_____

_____

_____

Did you know: (optional) _____

_____

_____

_____

Comparisons: (optional) _____

_____

_____

_____

Other: _____

_____

_____

_____

Next Meeting Date, Time, Location _____

_____

BARGAINING MINUTES

Date of Session: _____

Starting Time: _____ Ending Time: _____

Present for the Association:

_____
Spokesperson

_____
Recorder

Present for Management:

_____
Spokesperson

Notation of Association proposals (copies attached):

Notation of Management proposals (copies attached):

Notation of Tentative Agreements (copies attached/signed):

Note: Original handwritten/computer generated minutes (stored in two places), along with attachments should be kept on permanent file.

Page _____ of _____ pages

Date _____

Person Speaking

Other Notations   Record of Discussion

TENTATIVE AGREEMENT CONCEPTS

1. It is difficult to recall all the conversations that take place during negotiations, so it is imperative that some designated member(s) of the team take notes (a computer is the best option) during each bargaining session.

2.Discussions and agreements on proposals must be noted as they happen. The most important record of all is the Tentative Agreement, a written account of the provisions contained in the settlement:

    A. It should be signed by the Parties and become the basis of a formal contract.

    B. The negotiations should not end until all provisions have been resolved and a Tentative Agreement has been signed with copies to both negotiation teams.

    C. Whoever writes the agreement has an advantage, so keep your own records.

3. Be prepared to take the following precautions:

    A. The Tentative Agreement should be read carefully by more than one person to eliminate errors of omission and commission.

    B. If you do not like the wording, rewrite it.

    C. No matter how late the hour, do not sign the memo until it reflects the agreement exactly as you understand it.

5. Two ways to administrate the Tentative Agreement:

    *A. Both Parties sign two separate Tentative Agreements, and each retains original copy.

    B. Both Parties sign one copy, then photo copy two additional copies and destroy the original.

    *Preferred and safest approach

Example of Tentative Agreement

Article III

Section 8 – Personal Leave

1. Employees shall be entitled to three days personal leave annually.

2. Such leave may be used for personal matters conducted during regular business hours.

3. Such leave is non-accumulative.

<u>Tentative Agreement (TA)</u>

<u>Ulysses Abamo</u>	<u>12-19-09</u>	<u>Josephine Hussein</u>
Association	Date	Management

LOCAL BARGAINING PLAN
BARGAINING SEQUENCE

1. Select a team that represents a cross section of members such as departments, areas, special interest groups, etc.
2. Analyze the existing contract for problem areas.
3. Survey members, collect, analyze data, and identify issues.
4. Establish goals and settlement standards for each issue.
5. Rate issues 1, 2, and 3, with most important being 1.
6. Rank unresolved issues within category (1, 2, and 3) with 1 being the most important and 3 being the least important, or some other team-endorsed scheme.
7. Prepare package using boilerplate or prototype with the highest reasonable standards to frame initial bargaining positions and do not copy already compromised language from other contracts.
8. Bargain non-economic issues rated 3 first, then 2 and finally 1 last.
9. Generally speaking, economic issues are normally bargained last and/or as a package.
10. Begin discussions on #1 non-economic rated issues by a specified date in order to emphasize and devote sufficient time and energy to the important issues and prevent getting pressured for time at closure or prior to a deadline date.

ESTABLISHING GOALS AND SETTLEMENT STANDARDS

	ISSUE	GOAL*	SETTLEMENT STANDARD*
1.			
2.			
3.			
4.			
5.			
6.			
7.			
8.			
9.			

Goal: Preferred position.
Settlement Standard: Acceptable position for settlement.

*Goals and Settlement Standards can be the same.

BACKGROUND FOR ESTABLISHING GOALS AND SETTLEMENT STANDARDS

Instructions:
1. Break up into designated teams (2 or 3 trainees).
2. The Association represents all members.
3. The Association team has to determine a goal and settlement standard for each issue based on the information below in the last two columns.
4. The teams will make decisions based on sufficient consensus.
5. There are no right or wrong answers.

Issue	Goal(s)*	Settlement Standard(s)*	Current Contract	Comparison for other similar Local/area Contracts
Personal Leave			None	2-4 days
Association Leave			None	35-40 days
Family Illness			None	3-5 days
Emergency Leave			None	3-4 days
Vacations			5 days	15-20 days
Holidays			10 days	12 days
Paternity Leave			None	1 day
Jury Duty/ Court Duty			Silent	Excused w/ full pay

*Can be the same.

ISSUE RATING
BARGAINING ANALYSIS GUIDE

#1 Rated Issues (Most Important)	#2 Rated Issues	#3 Rated Issues (Least Important)
1)	1)	1)
2)	2)	2)
3)	3)	3)
4)	4)	4)
5)	5)	5)
6)	6)	6)
7)	7)	7)
8)	8)	8)
9)	9)	9)
10)	10)	10)

ISSUE RATING EXERCISE

Instructions
1.   Utilize the same teams.
2.   Rate the following issues #1-2-3 and list them under each category by sufficient consensus, using the same assumptions as previously.
3.   There are no right or wrong answers.

1. Association President's released time	5. Mileage Reimbursement	9. Training Funds
2. Salary/Wages	6. Seniority based layoff	
3. Fringe Benefits	7. Sexual Harassment	
4. Paid Holidays	8. Jury Duty/Court Duty	

#1 Rated Issues
(Most Important)

#2 Rated Issues

#3 Rated Issues
(Least Important)

41

ISSUE RANKING EXERCISE WORKSHEET

Instructions
1. Utilize the same teams.
2. Using the same assumptions, take the same issues you rated and rank them within each category below.
3. There are no right or wrong answers.
4. Use sufficient consensus to make decisions.

#1 Rated Issues (Most Important)	#2 Rated Issues	#3 Rated Issues (Least Important)
1.1. (top half)	2.1 (top half)	3.1 (top half)
1.2 (bottom half)	2.2 (bottom half)	3.2 (bottom half)

BARGAINING BLUEPRINT GUIDE

Ranking listed in order of importance

Rated Issues	Goal	Settlement Standard
#1 Rated Issues		
1.1		
1.2		
#2 Rated Issues		
2.1		
2.2		
#3 Rated Issues		
3.1		
3.2		

LOCAL BARGAINING FRAMEWORK FOR ISSUE RATING AND RANKING

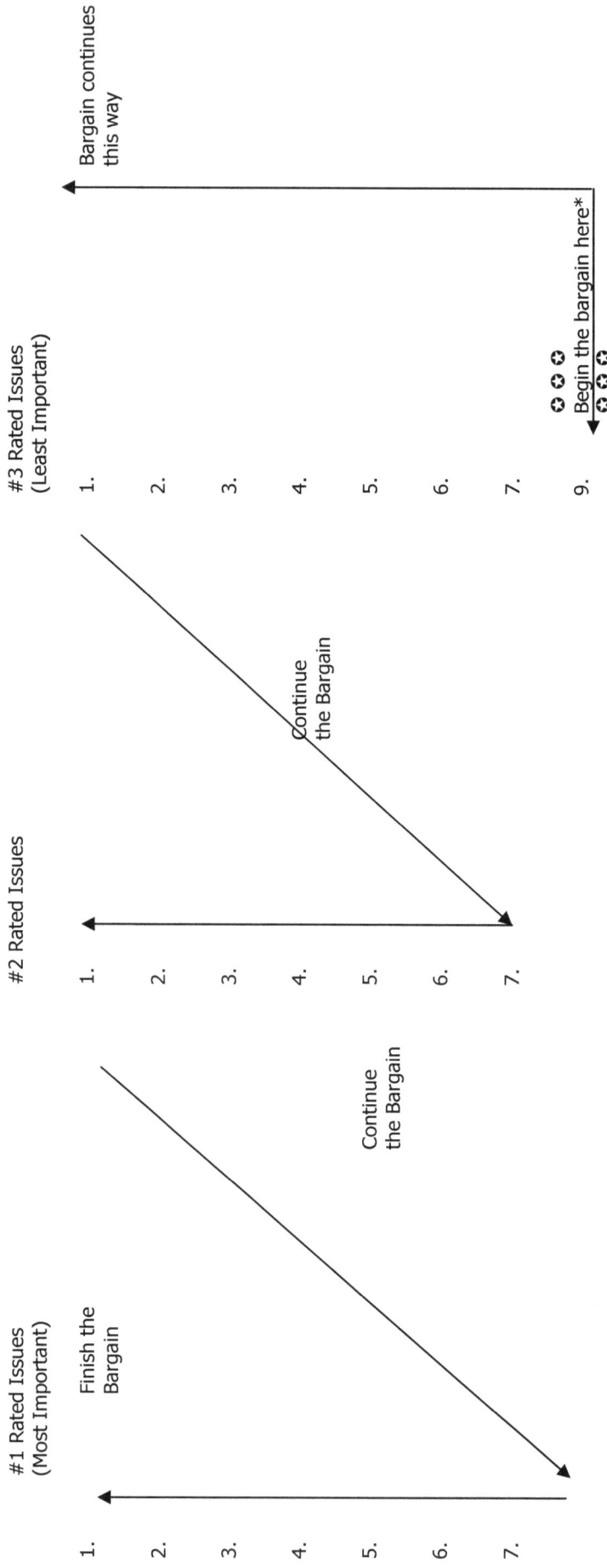

#1 Rated Issues (Most Important)

1. Finish the Bargain
2.
3.
4.
5.
6.
7.

#2 Rated Issues

1.
2.
3.
4. Continue the Bargain
5.
6.
7.

#3 Rated Issues (Least Important)

1.
2.
3.
4.
5. Continue the Bargain
6.
7.
9. Begin the bargain here*

Bargain continues this way

Prioritization of issues within each category from most important (#1) to least important (#3).

✪ ✪

Normally the low rated, low ranked non-economic issues are bargained first and the economic issues bargained last usually in a package. The last package may be a mix of non-economic and economic issues.

44

ANALYZING ISSUES AND/OR PACKAGES

Settlement Scale

+++	Meets goal	O	Little or no impact
++	Meets settlement standard	-	Minor loss or change with little or no impact
+	Some improvement	--	Major substantive loss

Issue Last Management Offer	Goal*	Settlement Standard*	Settlement Scale or Analysis
1.			
2.			
3.			
4.			
5.			
6.			
7.			
8.			

Goal is the preferred position. Settlement Standard is an acceptable position for settlement.
*Goal and Settlement Standard can be the same.

ANALYZING ISSUES OR PACKAGES IN BARGAINING

Issue	Existing Contract	Goal	Settlement Standard	Last Management Offer	Analyze Last Management Offer +++, ++, +, 0,-, --
Association Leave	5 days	20 days	15 days	19 days	
Personal Leave	1 day	3 days	2 days	2 days	
Union Security Clause	Grandfathered	Full	Same	Delete from contract	
Paid Holidays	None	Add 2	Add 1	2 new holidays	
Emergency Days	1 day	4 days	3 days	5 days	
Vacations	None	7 days	5 days	4 days at Christmas	
Association Office Rent	$100 per year	No change	No change	$110 per year	
Employee Parking	$10 per month	Free	Free	$5 per month	
Sick Leave	10 annual	14 annual	12 annual	13 annual	
Bereavement Leave	3 days	5 days	5 days	4 days	

Settlement Scale

+++	Meets goal
++	Meets settlement standard
+	Some improvement
O	Little or no impact
-	Minor loss or change with little or no impact
--	Major substantive loss

CASE STUDIES FOR PACKAGE ANALYSIS

1. Bargaining Analysis Case Study #1

Management has given the Association an <u>eleven-issue</u> "Settlement Offer," and the bargaining team has analyzed their offer with the following results:

    1. 5 of the #1 rated issues are +++
    2. 4 of the #2 rated issues are ++
    3. 2 of the #3 rated issues are +

    Where is the Association in terms of settlement?
    Close?
    Not close?
    What should the team do after the analysis?

2. Bargaining Analysis Case Study #2

Management has presented the Association with a "Last and Best Settlement Offer" on <u>seventeen outstanding issues</u>. The Association analyzed the package with the following results:

    1. 5 of the #3 rated issues were +++
    2. 4 of the lowest rated #2 issues were ++
    3. 4 of the highest rated #2 issues were +
    4. 4 of the #1 rated issues were 0

    Where is the Association in terms of settlement?
    Close?
    Not close?
    What should the team do after the analysis?

Blank Notation Page

SMALL PACKAGE BLUEPRINT: 10-15 ISSUES

Rated Issues	Goal	Settlement Standard	Final Settlement	Analysis (+++. ++, +, 0, -, --)
#1 Rated Issues 1				
2				
Rankings listed by 3				
rank order of 4				
importance 5				
6				
#2 Rated Issues 1				
2				
3				
4				
5				
#3 Rated Issues 1				
2				
3				
4				

MEDIUM PACKAGE BLUEPRINT: 20-30 ISSUES

Rated Issues	Goal	Settlement Standard	Final Settlement	Analysis +++. ++, +, 0, -, --
#1 Rated Issues				
1.1 (top third)				
Rankings listed by rank order of importance				
1.2 (middle third)				
1.3 (bottom third)				
#2 Rated Issues 2.1				
2.2				
2.3				
#3 Rated Issues 3.1				
3.2				
3.3				

50

LARGE PACKAGE BLUEPRINT

Rated Issues	Goal	Settlement Standard	Final Settlement	Analysis +++. ++, +, 0, -, --
#1 Rated Issues				
Rankings listed by rank order of importance	1.1 (top half)			
	2.1(bottom half)			
#2 Rated Issues	2.1			
	2.2			
#3 Rated Issues	3.1			
	3.2			

51

ANY SIZE PACKAGE BLUEPRINT

Rated Issues	Goal	Settlement Standard	Final Settlement	Analysis +++. ++, +, 0, -, --
#1 Rated Issues	1.1 Economic			
Rankings listed by rank order of importance	1.2 Non-Economic			
#2 Rated Issues	2.1 Economic			
	2.2 Non-Economic			
#3 Rated Issues	3.1 Economic			
	3.2 Non-Economic			

BARGAINING PREPARTION PLANNING AND TRACKING INSTRUMENT

Issue	Goal	Settlement Standard Timeline	Opening Position	1st Fallback/ Timeline	2nd Fallback/ Timeline	3rd Fallback/ Timeline	Analysis +++. ++, +, 0, -, --
#1 Rated Issues							
1.1							
1.2							
1.3							
#2 Rated Issues							
2.1							
2.2							
2.3							
#3 Rated Issues							
3.1							
3.2							
3.3							

53

BE AWARE

Teams with high expectations bargained better contracts than those with low expectations.

1. Teams with low expectations realize their expectations.

2. Deadlines, real or perceived, force decisions and ultimately settlements.

3. Make the Board bargain up to your goal and/or settlement standard.

4. Bargaining teams have problems when they are more concerned with the relationship of the Parties than meeting the needs of their members.

5. Teams experience major problems trying to bargain free lance, without a consensus-driven bargaining blueprint.

6. Finally, teams with a blueprint who do not follow it are likely to have serious internal team problems, along with concerns from the members and leaders.

7. Be aware of teams without patience who want to tell the other Party the "bottom line" in order to get an agreement settled as soon as possible and go home.

"ONE PASS THROUGH" STRATEGY

When members want issues bargained that will be extremely difficult or impossible to achieve, we utilize a "One Pass Through" strategy and designate it "OPT" in the blueprint.

The team makes at least one good faith effort to bargain the issue with Management.

In the event Management says no, then we let the issue die and drop it in the final stages of bargaining.

This positions the organization on the right side of the issue and protects us with our members by forcing Management to reject the proposal, rather than the Association refusing to bargain the issue.

This strategically is better than having the Association refusing to bargain the issue because we tried and Management said no.

FRAMEWORK OF AN INITIAL OPENING STATEMENT FIRST MEETING

1. Introduce all team members and respective constituency groups.

2. Make some general statements the team is committed to:

   a. Bargaining in good faith.

   b. Reaching a fair and equitable agreement.

   c. Settling within a reasonable time frame.

   d. Using a problem-solving approach.

3. Ascertain their team has the authority to reach agreements at the table without going back to the Board.

EXERCISE FOR OPENING POSITION - BACKGROUND

The Association membership has identified the following issues for bargaining. The bargaining team has decided on the goals and settlement standards.

Issue Standard	Goal	Settlement Standard
Salary/Wage	3%	2%
Training Finds employee	$350 per employee	$250 per employee
Holidays	Add Martin Luther King Day	Same
Personal Leave	Add two days	Add one day

Exercise

The Association's first offer (opening position) on each issue is as follows:

1. Salary/Wage _____

2. Training Funds _____

3. Holidays _____

4. Personal Leave _____

BASIC COUNTERPROPOSAL CONCEPTS

1. Concede slowly at every stage of the bargain.

2. Make sure there is a "quid pro quo" for all individual issue/package agreements.

3. Asking several questions and having lengthy discussions on any Management issues sends a signal your team is willing to consider making a change.

4. When in doubt, fall back to "No" as a strategy.

5. If it is written and signed by the Parties, it is worth something.

6. If it is a promise, it is worth nothing.

7. When in doubt, resubmitting your previous proposal, without apology, is always an option.

STATUS QUO COUNTERSTRATEGIES

Counters/Responses to maintain the status quo:

1. Listen attentively to what the other Party has to say and then "Dead Space."

2. Be prepared to filibuster and talk at length, even if it means different people repeating the same "No" message several times in a variety of ways.

   a. Explain why and how the deal will be detrimental to both Parties.

   b. Resubmit your previous proposals without much explanation.

3. Develop a counter with some insignificant movement on one or two low rated issues.

4. A straight "No" is always an option.

ESSENTIALS FOR WRITING PROPOSALS AND COUNTERS

1. Start at the highest reasonable position so there is plenty of room to negotiate and wait for the other Party to make the first major concession.

2. Be aware of the needs, goals, and settlement standards, and rating and ranking, on any issue in the blueprint at all times.

3. Work off your own proposal.

4. Test language to make sure it is:

   a. Clear and concise.

   b. Enforceable in the grievance procedure.

5. Make sure there is sufficient consensus for every decision.

BLUNDERS IN WRITING PROPOSALS AND COUNTERPROPOSALS

1. Copying already compromised language from other contracts.

2. Making the initial proposal either too close to the goal or settlement standard without sufficient room to bargain.

3. Failing to have a clear position on either goals or settlement standards at a given point in time.

4. Failing to get Management's real objections or rationale before responding.

5. Giving away too much too fast is a sign of weakness.

6. Accepting the first offer, unless it meets or is very close to a goal.

7. Not understanding your needs. The key question is, "Does this new proposal meet our needs?"

COUNTERPROPOSAL EXERCISE

Background: The Association and Management have been negotiating personal leave. You are the Association team.

Association Information:

Current Contract: silent
Goal: 4 days
Area Standard for other similar contracts: 3 days
Settlement Standard: 2 days
Opening Position: 6 days
Current Position: 6 days
Rating: 2
Ranking: 2.2
Language for Association Current Opening Position is as follows:

> Every employee shall have six (6) personal leave days with pay per year to be used for personal or family matters that require absence during work hours. The applicant shall not be required to state the reason for taking leave.

Management has just given the Association team the following counter:

> Each employee in the bargaining unit is entitled to use one day of personal leave without loss of pay; provided, however, leave will not be granted the day before or after holidays, vacations, or sick days, and is non-accumulative.

The Association team has received the Management proposal. Management considers this a generous offer considering for years their response has been a flat no.

Instructions:

Prepare a written association counterproposal on the next page based on this information.

Counter No. _____

Date _____

Time_____

COUNTERPROPOSAL BACKGROUND AND EXERCISE SHEET

The members have identified the following issues for bargaining. The bargaining team has decided on the goals and settlement standards.

Issue	Goal	Settlement Standard
Vandalism Fund	$10,000 pool for bargaining unit	$6,000 pool for bargaining unit
Salary/Wages	5.00%	3.00%
Holidays	Add Martin Luther King Day as a paid holiday	Same as goal
Training Funds	$50,000 pool for bargaining unit	Get a fund started
Association Leave	50 paid days for bargaining unit	25 days

Instructions

1. Develop a written counterproposal within a conceptual framework based on the above information for each of the issues.

2. The Association's first offer was as follows:

    A. Vandalism Fund - $20,000 pool.
    B. Training Funds- $85,000 pool.
    C. Association Leave 100 days paid leave.
    D. Salary/Wage-10%.
    E. Holidays- add Martin Luther King as a paid holiday.

3.   Management's last offer was as follows:

    A. Vandalism Fund - $5,000 for bargaining unit.
    B. Training Funds - $55,000 for bargaining unit.
    C. Association Leave- NO!
    D. Salary/Wage- 2%.
    E. Holidays- add Martin Luther King as an unpaid holiday.

4. Develop an Association strategy and a written Association counterproposal for the Management's last offer on the next page.

1. Association Strategy:

2. Association Counterproposal:

STRATEGIES FOR RESPONDING TO REGRESSIVE
OR NEGATIVE PROPOSALS

1. Caucus and rethink your strategy.

2. Counter escalate. Raise your offer or demand. Respond to unreasonable positions with your own unreasonable demands or reintroduce opening positions to test the other team's strength and resolve.

3. Walk away from the offer.

4. Say, "No! No! No!"

5. Combinations of 1 – 4.

NEGATIVE OR REGRESSIVE PROPOSAL EXERCISE

Background

Management and the Association have been bargaining for several days, including the issue of training funds. You are the Association Team.

Association Information

Current Contract: $150 per employee
Goal: $250 per employee
Settlement Standard: $200 per employee
Opening Position: $400 per employee
Current Position: $375 per employee
Rating/Ranking: 2/5 of 10
Area Settlement Standard for other similar contracts: $245 per
    Employee

For the last several days, Management was offering an increase of $25 per employee, to $175 from the current contract. Recently, however, it was discovered that the Chief Financial Officer, who was immediately fired, overspent the budget. In order to make up this big deficit, Management's last proposal is to completely eliminate all training funds, so there would be no money whatsoever for training.

Instructions

1. Develop a written Association strategy as to what actions you would take.

2. Develop an appropriate written Association counterproposal.

3. Refer to worksheet on next page.

NEGATIVE OR REGRESSIVE PROPOSAL WORKSHEET

1. Association Strategy:

2. Association Counterproposal:

COUNTER STRATEGIES FOR NEGATIVE OR REGRESSIVE PROPOSALS

*Take-It-or-Leave-It Offers

*Last and Final Offers

*Sundown Offers with Artificial Deadlines

*Contingency offers that couple bad proposals so your team must agree to a bad Management proposal in order to get one or more Association priority issues.

1. The team, in a demonstration of unity, can abruptly leave without notice and report back to the Association Executive Board.

2. Your team could submit their own Last and Final Offer within the guidelines of the blueprint, with sufficient room to bargain.

3. The team can take the offer back to share with the membership, with a recommendation to reject.

4. Management's proposal should be cross-checked with the Association blueprint to identify the major problems in their proposal.

5. New alternatives and possible solutions should be explored to develop a new counterproposal within the guidelines of the blueprint, plus some flexibility to bargain.

6. If close, the shape of the package could be changed, including a comfortable cushion that gives the team several moves when drafting a counterproposal.

---

*The only real "last and best" or "last and final offer" is the one accepted by both parties – so do not be intimidated when presented with one.

LAST AND FINAL BACKGROUND

The Association and Management have successfully negotiated all issues except money, in-service, training, and Association leave.

Association Information

Issue: Money
Current Contract: 0
Goal: 8 percent
Area Standard for other similar contracts: 6.5 percent
Settlement Standard: 7 percent
Opening Position: 14 percent
Current Position: 12 percent

Goal: In-Service
Current Contract: silent
Goal: $250 per employee
Area Standard for other similar contracts: $150 per employee
Settlement Standard: $150 per employee
Opening Position: $500 per employee
Current Position: $300 per employee

Issue: Association Leave
Current Contract: silent
Goal: 50 days
Area Standard for other similar contracts: 45 days
Settlement Standard: 35 days
Opening Position: 80 days
Current Position: 65 days

Management has given the Association a true last and final, take it or leave it settlement proposal as follows:
- 5.5 percent money increase
- $125 per employee in-service
- 30 days Association leave

Instructions

1. Develop a written Association strategy to chart a course of action.

2. Develop an appropriate written Association counterproposal or response on the next page.

LAST AND FINAL EXERCISE

1. Association Strategy:

2. Association Counterproposal:

STAIR STEPPING PROPOSALS AT CLOSURE
FOR MULTI-YEAR AGREEMENTS

Single Issue, One Proposal

1.   Goal – the preferred settlement position.

2.   Settlement standards – gains or improvements that are acceptable in the short run, but do not meet goals.

Issue	Goal	Settlement Standard
Personal Leave	5 days	3 days

Example of How to Counter Propose by Stair Stepping at Closure

1st Year	2nd Year	3rd Year
3 days	4 days	5 days

STAIR STEPPING PROPOSALS AT CLOSURE FOR MULTI YEAR AGREEMENTS*

Single Issue, Three Counterproposals

Issue	Goal	Settlement Standard
Personal Leave	5 days	3 days

Example of How to Make Three Counterproposals at Closure

A. Settlement Proposal – Personal Leave

1st Year	2nd Year	3rd Year
3 days	5 days	6 days

B. Final Settlement Proposal

1st Year	2nd Year	3rd Year
3 days	4 days	6 days

C. Last and Final Offer

1st Year	2nd Year	3rd Year
3 days	4 days	5 days

*Try to anchor any reference to dollars in the contract to a percentage tied to the salary/wage schedule base, if possible, so it automatically increases every year without bargaining (____ percent of _____ base salary).

BACKGROUND INFORMATION SHEET FOR STAIRSTEPPING PROPOSALS AT CLOSURE FOR A MULTI-YEAR AGREEMENT

Option A

Issue	Current Association Position	Goal	Settlement Standard
Salary/Wage	14%	10%	8%
Association Leave	65 days	50 days	35 days
Family Illness	7 days	5 days	3 days
Vacation	30 days	15 days	12 Days

BACKGROUND RATING AND RANKING SHEET FOR HOW TO COUNTER AT CLOSURE BY STAIRSTEPPING

Option A

Instructions: Rate the following issues from #1- 3, and then rank from highest to lowest within each rating category.

		Settlement		
Issue	Goals	Standard	Rating	Ranking
Salary/Wage	10%	8%		
Association Leave	50 days	35 days		
Family Illness	5 days	3 days		
Vacation	15 days	12 days		

Then, transcribe below

#1 Rated Issues*   #2 Rated Issues   #3 Rated Issues

Ra
nki
ng
→

EXERCISE SHEET FOR STAIRSTEPPING PROPOSALS AT CLOSURE FOR MULTI-YEAR AGREEMENTS

Option A

Instructions:

- Organize into designated teams.
- The Association represents all members.
- The Association team has determined a goal and settlement standard for each issue based on the previous information.
- The teams will make decisions based on sufficient consensus.
- There are no right or wrong answers.
- Draft a settlement offer (first page), final settlement offer (second page) and last, best and final settlement offer (third page) offer based on the background sheet information.

SETTLEMENT PROPOSAL {Stair Step Proposal #1}

Issue	First Year	Second Year	Third Year
Salary/Wage			
Association Leave			
Family Illness			
Vacation			

EXERCISE SHEET FOR STAIRSTEPPING PROPOSALS AT CLOSURE
FOR MULTI-YEAR AGREEMENTS

Instructions: Draft a final settlement offer (this page) and last, best and final settlement offer (next page) based on the background sheet information.

FINAL SETTLEMENT PROPOSAL {Stair Step Proposal# 2}

Issue	First Year	Second Year	Third Year
Salary/Wage			
Association Leave			
Family Illness			
Vacation			

EXERCISE SHEET FOR STAIRSTEPPING PROPOSALS AT CLOSURE FOR MULTI-YEAR AGREEMENTS

Option A

Instructions: Draft a last, best and final settlement offer below based on the background sheet information.

LAST, BEST AND FINAL SETTLEMENT PROPOSAL

Issue	First Year	Second Year	Third Year
Salary/Wage			
Association Leave			
Family Illness			
Vacation			

HOW TO COUNTER AT CLOSURE BY STAIRSTEPPING

Option B

- List unresolved issues to include rating (#1, 2, and 3) and ranking from most to least important within each rating category.

- All #1 rated issues should be effective in the first year, #2 rated items in the second year, and # 3 rated items in the third year.

- In the event Management does not respond to the #3 rated issues, counter propose a 2-year contract, and if Management does not want to bargain #2 rated issues, counter propose a one-year contract to force them to address all the issues.

LAST, BEST, and FINAL OFFER FOR A 3-YEAR CONTRACT		
1st Year	2nd Year	3rd Year
List #1 rated and/or highest ranked #2 rated issues	**List rest of #2** rated and/or highest rated #2 issues	**List #3 rated** issues and could include low ranked #2 issues

MINI PACKAGING CONCEPTS

Consider a mini package with 3-rated issues or one specific article and/or section of the contract.

Consider a mini package with 2- and 3-rated issues.

Package the remainder of 1, 2, and 3 unresolved issues.

Review needs, goals, and settlement standards if the team reaches an internal impasse, or prior to giving Management the package.

Include some "bait" or something in the proposal that would be of interest to Management and will be acceptable to members, as long as it is compatible with the goals and/or settlement standards in the blueprint.

MINI PACKAGING EXERCISE

The Association and Management have been bargaining for several weeks. The Association represents all members. The following facts are pertinent to the exercise.

Issue	Association Goal	Standard for other similar area contracts	Association Settlement Standard	Association Opening Position	Association Current Position	Last Management Offer	Association Rating/ Ranking
Salary/Wages	8%	6%	6%	12%	10%	4.5%	1/1
Personal Leave	3 days	2 days	2 days	5 days	4 days	1 day	3/1
Family Leave	3 days	3 days	3 days	5 days	5 days	2 days	3/3
Holidays	12 days	11 days	10 days	14 days	14 days	10 days	¼
Insurance	+10%	+8%	+7.5%	+14%	+14%	7%	½
Bereavement Leave	5 days	4 days	3 days	7 days	5 days	3 days	3/5
Emergency Leave	3 days	3 days	3 days	5 days	4 days	1 day	3/7
Association Leave	40 days	30 days	25 days	65 days	60 days	32 days	3/10

The bargaining is headed for the final stages and Management has begun to deal in packages. The Association is next to draft a counterproposal. Labor relations have generally been good over the years, as each party has attempted to bargain in "good faith" to reach an agreement.

Instructions

* Separate the issues into two different "mini packages" of similar type issues.
* Draft two different written mini packages using all the specified issues with appropriate labels.

**Management has some grave concerns about the following issues:

1. Bereavement Leave – cannot be used outside the immediate family.
2. Association Leave – Association must pay cost of substitute.
3. Personal Leave – Cannot be used for recreation, vacation, or profit.
4. Insurance – Management wants to select company/carrier.

Counter No. _____ Mini Package #1
Date _____

Time _____

Counter No. _____ Mini Package #2

Date _____

Time _____

MINI PACKAGE EXERCISE SHEET
OPTION B

Instructions: Based on the rating and ranking in the previous mini packaging exercise, prepare two settlement offers based on a three-year contract utilizing Option B.

FINAL SETTLEMENT PROPOSAL

First Year   Second Year   Third Year

LAST, BEST AND FINAL SETTLEMENT PROPOSAL

First Year   Second Year   Third Year

Information is power
Skilled bargainers are deep listeners

TWO GENERAL TYPES OF QUESTIONS

Open-ended: requires an explanation in order to gather information.

"What are your problems with our proposal?"

"Can you explain the impact of this proposal?"

Closed-ended: requires a "Yes" or "No" answer or generally a very limited response.

"Will the Board ratify this agreement?"

"Are we at tentative agreement on this package?"

Through the use of questions, a good bargainer can control the dialog at the table while at the same time causing the other party to do *most* of the talking. Remember, information is power.

THREE TYPES OF QUESTIONS IN SEQUENCE

1. Information Seeking: A What Question

   Association bargainer's original question begins with "what" identifies the information area.

   Example: "What are your real objections to our proposal?"

2. Clarifying: A What Do You Mean or What Do You Have In Mind Question

   Association bargainer's second question assures you understand the answers by giving clarity.

   Example: "When you say 'make every effort', what do you mean?"

3. Justifying (rationale-asking question): A Why Question

   Association bargainer's third question asks to explain why their proposal would be fairer, better, more practical, less costly and/or more beneficial.

   Example: "How can we convince our members to ratify a contract that eliminates seniority-based transfer?"

QUESTIONING SKILLS:
THE MOST IMPORTANT PART OF BARGAINING

Why Questioning?

1. A truly effective bargain involves both Parties asking and answering a series of questions to seek information and not much filibustering (speech making).

2. Bargaining is not a speech and/or debate process. The bargaining involves intensive question and answer dialogue until there is a "meeting of the minds."

3. Question the bargain to closure. An observer at the table should be able to visualize the settlement by listening to the questions and answers of both Parties without looking at the blueprints.

4. Listen for new information. Skilled bargainers are good listeners. You should do twice as much listening after asking discovery questions. An effective bargainer can control the dialogue at the table by asking questions and causing the other Party to do most of the talking. Information is power.

STRATEGIES FOR ENTRAPMENT QUESTIONS

1. "Would you repeat the question using another frame of reference?"

2. "Explain the question again in detail using different examples, since it is not clear."

3. Dead space the question and move on to the next issue.

4. "Our team needs clarification and more information, so our position remains unchanged at this time."

5. "Your question is so confusing and so misleading that it would be in our best interests to move on to the next issue and work toward settlement."

6. "Your question and the information we have from our impacted members are in direct conflict, so we are wasting our time."

ADVANCED NEGOTIATION SKILLS

1.   Kick Start Questions

     "What parts of our proposal are acceptable?"

2.   Zero In Questions

     "Identify the specific parts of our proposal that are unacceptable."

3.   Split the Baby Offers

     We can make the issue acceptable for both parties by proposing an agreement to someplace in the high middle of both Parties' proposals as long as it stays within the guidelines of our blueprint.

     Strategy: Always stay above where you want to settle so it is a "high split" of the baby.

4.   Coupling or Hook and Ladder Offers

     "I won't agree to this proposal unless you agree to these Proposals."

     "We will withdraw our Article 40 if you withdraw your Article 45."

     "We will agree to your money proposal parts if you will agree to our fully paid insurance proposal."

ADVANCED NEGOTIATION STRATEGIES

5. Hostage and Ransom Strategy

    Teams hold an issue "hostage." Management sometimes will hold the union security clause (fair share, representation fee, or agency fee) and/or binding arbitration hostage, then make proposals to restore it to the contract if we agree to drop a few of our proposals that are unacceptable to them.

    Strategy: The Association should consider getting a "hostage," like the Management Rights Clause, and do a quid pro quo hostage release later in the bargain.

6. Mirror Strategy

    Whenever presented with an anti-employee or anti-Association clause, simply turn it around and place the burden on the other Party.

    Management Proposal: The Association will never engage in or condone a strike or work stoppage for the duration of the contract.

    Association Counter: Management will not lockout employees for the duration of the contract.

> **When the Parties reach verbal or conceptual agreements or understandings, the Association should always write its own version and present it to Management.**

ADVANCED NEGOTIATIONS SKILLS EXERCISES

Kick Start

Instructions: Identify and underline the following parts of this Management proposal that are <u>acceptable.</u>

Every employee shall be granted three days personal leave per year non accumulative; provided, however, personal leave will not be granted for recreational, social, fraternal, or personal profit. The employees will be required to state in writing the reasons for the leave.

Zero In

Instructions: Identify and cross out the specific parts of this Management proposal that are <u>unacceptable</u>.

Every employee in the bargaining unit will be granted two days of personal leave annually; provided, however, it will not be granted the first or last five days of classes or the day before or after vacations or holidays; provided further, the employee will give two weeks' advance notice. The leave will be granted for personal business that requires absence during work hours.

Split the Baby

Instructions: Devise a strategy utilizing verbal skills as to how you would attempt to close out this issue.

Management has offered $100 per employee for training, and the Association has a proposal for $250 per employee for training on the table. The Association goal is $175 per employee, and the settlement standard is $150 per employee. This is one of the last proposals that is holding up the Agreement.

Coupling, or Hook and Ladder

The following are proposals by each Party that are left on the table in the final stages of bargaining. How would you couple these proposals to bring about closure? Draw arrows to designate how issues could be coupled.

Association	Current Contract	Management
Association Office Space	Silent	The right to suspend in case of serious charges against employee.
Just Cause	Silent	The Association will pay cost of substitutes.
Association Leave	Silent	Nominal rental fee

Hostage and Ransom

Instructions: Devise an association strategy to counter this tactic.

Management has proposed in its initial bargaining package to delete the binding arbitration clause. In the past, the Management bargainer has used this holding of an important Association issue hostage in other contract negotiations. Late in the bargain, she will try to get the Association team to drop some important proposals in exchange for releasing the binding arbitration hostage. She has been very successful utilizing this strategy in the past.

Mirror

Instructions: Devise an Association counterproposal in bargaining to the following Management proposal.

The Association had the unlimited opportunity to make, assess, and analyze proposals during bargaining. Therefore, the Association waives its right and relieves Management of its obligation to bargain on any new issues during the term of this contract.

Management and the association just reached a conceptual agreement on personal leave at the end of a long day of bargaining. Both Parties are tired. What should the Association do now?

UTILIZING "WHAT IF" STRATEGY

Supposals, especially in mediation

1."What if" questions are used to explore possible alternatives, concessions, compromises consistent with Association goals, and/or settlement standards that may be beneficial to both Parties. They are called "supposals."

*2. "Supposals" are useful for discussing the possible coupling of issues, packaging, or trading items of mutual interest designed to break deadlocks without officially committing to them at the table.

*3. "Supposals" enable teams to change the shape of the package without changing the size of the package.

4. Examples: "If we agreed to accept your proposal to prohibit personal leave during the first five days and the last five days of the year, would you agree to add another day?"

*This strategy is often used in a "pencils down," no-record-keeping discussion to explore possibilities for breaking an impasse and can be used effectively with a mediator carrying the message.

EXERCISE #1 FOR "WHAT IF" STRATEGY

Change the Shape of the Package

Background
Current Positions of Parties

Issue	Association	Management
Salary/Wages ($50,000)	+10% ($100,000)	+5%
Insurance ($15,000)	10% ($30,000)	+5%
Training Funds ($5,000)	+10% ($10,000)	+5%
Material & Equipment, Supplies Fund ($2,500)	+10% ($5,000)	+5%

The bargaining process is nearing closure. Management commits $108,000 in new money to the bargaining table and asks the Association if it can shape the money into a final settlement. Management has agreed to commit the resources; now the Association has to decide on how to shape the money into a package so the team can determine whether or not it can work with the offer.

Association Bargaining Blueprint

	Goal (New Money)	Settlement Standard (New Money)
1. Salary/Wages	8% ($80,000)	6% ($60,000)
2. Insurances	8% ($24,000)	6% ($18,000)
3. Training Funds	8% ($ 8,000)	6% ($ 6,000)
4. Materials, Equipment, Supplies Fund	8% ($ 4,000)	6% ($ 3,000)

Instructions

You are the Association team, and it is your responsibility to determine the final package to present to Management for mutual approval and eventually to the Association membership at the ratification meeting.

Develop a written, cost designated final proposal to present to Management on the next page.

Lessons learned?

EXERCISE SHEET #1 FOR "WHAT IF" OR SUPPOSAL STRATEGY

Association Settlement Proposal

SUPPOSAL STRATEGY BACKGROUND #2

The Association and Management are discussing personal leave at the table. The following information is pertinent to the bargaining. The Parties are in mediation, and there is a mediator present during bargaining. The Parties are deadlocked on this issue. The Association has five personal leave days on the table, and Management has utilized a dead space strategy to date on this issue.

Association Information

Goal is three days, like other, similar contracts.
Settlement standard is two days as a minimum.
Members do not want to give reasons.
Members will not pay any costs.

Management Information

Willing to discuss parity with other similar industries.
Would like cost of substitute paid by employee.
Does not desire that days be used to extend holidays or vacations.
Will absolutely not allow these days to be used for recreation purposes. There is a nationally renowned ski area within ten miles, and when employees are not at work and are seen skiing that day, the company Board of Directors "goes ballistic."
Management wants reasons given to make sure days are not used for recreational purposes.

Instructions: Develop a written Association counterproposal to be given orally to a mediator as a "What If" proposal to Management utilizing creative solutions to break the deadlock—without committing to them at the table. The proposal should meet the guidelines for goals and/or settlement standards established on the blueprint for this issue.

ASSOCIATION SETTLEMENT PROPOSAL

BASIC TENETS OF "VOICE" IN DECISION-MAKING

1. The Parties determine the composition and number of representatives from each constituent group.

2. Our members have a seat with authentic participation and a voice in the decision making process.

3. Our Association selects its own representatives.

4. Our members have an equal or significant (majority) voice in decision making.

5. Our members are present and participate in the final decisions.

6. The decision-making climate is free of fear and intimidation.

7. If a consensus model is used and consensus is reached, all Parties agree to support the decision and work toward implementation.

8. If you are either late or absent, you consent.

9. The process always moves forward and will not be revisited for any anyone or any reason.

10. The first order of business is to agree on a decision making process, which cannot be changed.

BARGAINING PILLARS AND POSTS

Generally Speaking—

1. "Bargaining strong" by tracking and following a consensus-driven blueprint normally results in excellent settlements.

2. "Bargaining scared" results in poor settlements.

3. "Bargaining smart" means being aware of and considering all the internal and external forces in play and knowing when to settle the contract.

4. "Bargaining strong and smart" will produce +++ settlements.

SIMULATIONS

The author has copies of training simulations available for K-12, (certificated and classified), community college (full time, part time, and classified), and higher education. Contact information is on the last page of this book.

GENERIC

BARGAINING ESSENTIALS

HOW TO SUCCESSFULLY BARGAIN FROM SURVEY TO SETTLEMENT AND MAXIMIZE YOUR WINS

FINAL SIMULATION

ASSOCIATION PACKET

Group #1 Management	Joint Meeting Room	Table 1 Association
Group #2 Management	Joint Meeting Room	Table 2 Association
Group #3 Management	Joint Meeting Room	Table 3 Association
Group #4 Management	Joint Meeting Room	Table 4 Association

GENERAL INSTRUCTIONS: ALL TRAINEES

Pick up your training information and go to your caucus room to start preparing for the simulation.

Trainee packets for Association and Management teams will be distributed so make sure you have the right packet.

The target time frame to start the bargain is between_____ _____ and no later than

_____.

There is a copy machine available in_____.

The final completion deadline time is

_____.

BACKGROUND: ASSOCIATION

Date of Current Bargaining Session: August 29

Contract expires: September 1

Size of Industry: Medium

100 production employees

Business Revenue: $10,000,000

Cash Balance: $1,000,000 (10%)

History of Labor Relations:

1. Association bargains for 100 skilled employees.

2. Association leaders are viewed as moderates in the community.

3. Labor relations between the parties have generally been positive.

4. There have been ten bargaining sessions to date.

5. Management has moved very little in last three sessions.

6. The Association has a general membership meeting scheduled for September 1, 5:00 p.m. to discuss either ratification or a potential job action.

Community Background: The majority of patrons work under private, local, county, state, or federal collective bargaining agreements. There is a shortage of qualified labor. The Association members and leaders are active in local politics and community organizations.

* Both teams have the exact same background information.

FINAL SIMULATION: ASSOCIATION

Unresolved Issues	Contract Standards for other local Associations in similar size/type industries	Current Contract
Personal Leave	3 days	1 day
Compensation	3%	3% bargained previous 3 years
Holidays	New Year's Day and Christmas Day are paid holidays	Nonexistent
Association Leaves	22 days	5 days paid by Management
Special Equipment	$150 per employee per year	None

Positions of the Parties:

Association

        Personal Leave – 5 days.
        Compensation – 6%.
        Paid Holidays – add Christmas and New Year's Day.
        Union Leave – 40 days.
        Special Equipment Fund - $300 per employee per year.

Management

        Personal Leave – current contract, plus add new language stating cannot be used for the day before or after vacations and holidays.
        Compensation –1%.
        Paid Holidays –No.
        Association Leave – 5 days, Association pays cost of replacement (if necessary), benefits, and retirement.
        Special Equipment Fund – create an employee fund of $5,000 available on first come, first served basis with Management having final approval.

Teams:

Association	Management
1.	1.
2.	2.
3.	3.
4.	4.
5.	5.
6.	6.
7.	7.
8.	8.

Select teams and prepare accordingly to checklist below in caucus (use time efficiently).

1. Establish a team decision-making procedure.____
2. Establish method of communication at the table.____
3. Select a spokesperson for each issue and rotate so everyone has an opportunity to participate as much as possible. Any participant who is uncomfortable can decline the opportunity to be a spokesperson.____
4. Establish goals, settlement standards for each issue using bargaining analysis instrument on provided blueprint.____
5. Prepare brief opening statement and rationale.____
6. Utilize questioning techniques.____
7. Prepare for the bargain using the bargaining final blueprint.____

The skills, techniques and strategies that are to be utilized in the training simulation by the association team.

1. Bargaining will be in written proposals and counterproposals.____
2. Present one clearly regressive proposal on one issue.____
3. Present one last and final offer or all offers are withdrawn from the table.____

4. Agree and execute a minimum of one signed tentative agreement (see attached).____

5. Utilize "no" as a counterproposal at some point in time.__
6. Make one quick attempt at a "what if supposal" package during the last half hour to bring about closure.____

Keep It Simple (KISS) approach.

Debrief with both teams together.

Attachments:

        1.   Counterproposal sheets

        2.   Tentative Agreement sheets

        3.   Prototype (Boilerplate) starting language

        4.   Bargaining Blueprint Forms

The Association will make the first bargaining proposal in this exercise.

BARGAINING BACKGROUND SHEET

Issue	Opening Position	Current Position	Contract Standards for other nearby Local Industries of similar size/type**	Local Goal	Local Settlement Standard	Analysis +++, ++, +,0, -, --
Personal Leave	5 days	Same	3 days			
Compensation	6%	Same	3%			
Holidays	Add Christmas and New Year's paid holidays	Same	Association Position			
Association Leave	40 days	Same	22 days			
Special Equipment	$500 per employee per year	Same	$300 per employee per year			

*The Association team failed to establish goals and settlement standards. The original bargaining team resigned after the start of bargaining because of a dispute with the Association President. The first team never had time to develop a bargaining blueprint as a consequence of the political turmoil.

**The current team has reviewed the contract standards provided by the local labor council as stated in the information contract standards above and has decided to develop a blueprint in the best interests of team harmony.

FINAL BLUEPRINT

Rated Issues	Goal	Settlement Standard	Final Settlement	Analysis +++, ++, +, 0, -, --
#1 Rated Issues 1.1				
1.2				
#2 Rated Issues 2.1				
2.2				
#3 Rated Issues 3.1				
3.2				

+++ meets goal, ++ meets settlement standard, + improvement, 0 little/no impact, - minor loss, -- major loss

*This is an appropriate structure for a *small* package.

Association Bargaining Prototype Language
(Potential Initial Starting Positions)

Personal Leave

Employees shall have five personal leave days with pay per year to be used for matters which require absence during business hours. Notification shall be made, if possible, to the member's immediate supervisor for personal leave, except in cases of emergencies.

Union Leave

Management shall grant _____ days leave with pay to the Association to be used for business at the discretion of the Local President.

Special Equipment

Management will provide $_____ per year per employee for purchase of special work related equipment at the employee's discretion.

Counter No.   _____

Date   _____

Time   _____

115

Counter No. _____

Date _____

Time _____

Counter No. _____

Date _____

Time _____

TENTATIVE AGREEMENT

_____ _____ _____
For the Union   Date   For Management

TENTATIVE AGREEMENT

_____ _____ _____
For the Union   Date   For Management

TENTATIVE AGREEMENT

_____   _____   _____
For the Union   Date   For Management

OBSERVATION FORM FOR SIMULATION EXERCISE

As you observe this bargaining simulation, make appropriate notes for both teams on the following skills, tactics, techniques and strategies. Discuss your observations in the debrief following this simulation.

Bargaining Skills and Procedures	Association Team	Management Team
Team roles evident		
Team decision making process set and working		
Use of questioning skills		
Established goals and settlement standards		
Rated, ranked issues		
Utilized "no" as a response		
Had "flexibility" to bargain		
Worked off own proposal		
Met goals and settlement standards		

Notes:

_____

_____

_____

_____

TEAM DEBRIEF EXERCISE

1. Some team members should switch places at table so people are seated differently and effectively end the role playing.

2. What was your team decision-making process? What method did you use to achieve this end?

3. How did your team analyze and track the progress of the bargain?

4. What were your team's goals and settlement standards?

5. What were your team's settlement analysis results?

6. How would you rate your settlement in relationship to your goals and settlement standards?

7. Do you have any general comments about the experience?

GENERIC

BARGAINING ESSENTIALS

How to Successfully Bargain from Survey To Settlement and Maximize Your Wins

FINAL SIMULATION

MANAGEMENT PACKET

Group #1 Management	Joint Meeting Room	Table 1 Association
Group #2 Management	Joint Meeting Room	Table 2 Association
Group #3 Management	Joint Meeting Room	Table 3 Association
Group #4 Management	Joint Meeting Room	Table 4 Association

General Instructions: All Trainees

Pick up your training information and go to your caucus room to start preparing for the simulation.

Trainee packets for Association and Management teams will be distributed so make sure you have the right packet.

The target time frame to start the bargain is between_____
and no later than

_____.

There is a copy machine available
in_____.

The final completion deadline time is

_____.

BACKGROUND: MANAGEMENT

Date of Current Bargaining Session: August 29

Contract expires: September 1

Size of Industry: Medium

100 production employees

Business Revenue: $10,000,000

Cash Balance: $1,000,000 (10%)

History of Labor Relations:

> Association bargains for 100 skilled employees.
> Association leaders are viewed as moderates in the community.
> The labor relations between the parties have generally been positive.
> The Parties have met for ten bargaining sessions to date.
> Management has moved very little in last three sessions.
> Association has a general membership meeting scheduled for
> September 1, 5:00 P.M. to either ratify or discuss a possible job action.

Community Background: Majority of patrons work under private, local county, state, or federal collective bargaining agreements. There is a shortage of qualified labor. The Association members and leaders are active in local politics and community organizations.

* Both teams have the exact same background information.

FINAL SIMULATION: MANAGEMENT

Unresolved Issues	Contract Standards for other local industries of similar size/type	Current Contract
Personal Leave	3 days	1 day
Compensation	3%	3% received previous 3 years
Holidays	New Year's Day and Christmas Day are paid holidays	Nonexistent
Union Leaves	22 days	5 days paid by Management
Special Equipment	$150 per employee per year	None

Positions of the Parties:

Association

1. Personal Leave – 5 days.
2. Compensation -6%.
3. Paid Holidays – add Christmas and New Year's day.
4. Union Leave – 40 days.
5. Special Equipment Fund - $300 per employee per year.

Management

1. Personal Leave – current contract plus add new language stating cannot be used for the day before or after vacations and holidays.
2. Compensation – 1%.
3. Paid Holidays – No.
4. Association Leave – 5 days, The Association pays cost of replacement, if necessary, benefits and retirement.
5. Special Equipment Fund – create an employee fund of $5,000 available on first come, first served basis with Management having final approval.

Teams

	Association		Management
1.		1.	
2.		2.	
3.		3.	
4.		4.	
5.		5.	
6.		6.	
7.		7.	
8.		8.	

Select teams and prepare accordingly to checklist below in caucus (use time efficiently).

1. Establish a team decision-making procedure.____
2. Establish method of communication at the table.____
3. Select a spokesperson for each issue and rotate so everyone has an opportunity to participate as much as possible. Any participant who is uncomfortable can decline the opportunity to be a spokesperson.____
4. Establish goals, settlement standards for each issue using bargaining analysis instrument on provided blueprint.____
5. Prepare brief opening statement and rationale.____
6. Utilize questioning techniques.____
7. Prepare for the bargain using the bargaining final blueprint.____

The skills, techniques and strategies that are to be utilized in the training simulation by the Association team.

1. Bargaining will be in written proposals and counterproposals.____
2. Present one clearly regressive proposal on one issue.____
3. Present one last and final offer or all offers are withdrawn from the table.____
4. Agree and execute a minimum of one signed tentative agreement (see attached).____
5. Utilize "no" as a counterproposal at some point in time.__
6. Make one quick attempt at a "what if supposal" package during the last half hour to bring about closure.____

128

Keep It Simple (KISS) approach.

Debrief with both teams together.

Attachments:

        1.   Counterproposal sheets

        2.   Tentative Agreement sheets

        3.   Bargaining Blueprint Forms

        4. The Association will make the first bargaining proposal in this exercise.

BARGAINING SIMULATION BACKGROUND SHEET

Issue	Opening Position	Current Position	Research Standards for other Industries of similar size/type**	Management Approved Parameters	Analysis +++, ++, +,0, --
Personal Leave	1 days	1 days	3 days	2 or depending on the "right" package plus as many restrictions as possible	
Compensation	1%	1%	3%		
Holidays	No new paid holidays	No change	Most have Christmas and New Year's day as paid holidays	Will go to other Local industry standards depending on the "right" settlement package	
Union Leave	5 days	No change	22 days	Up to 20 days and Union pays replacement employee wages/costs	
Special Equipment	No	Same	$100 per employee per year	Control issue with management approval	

*The Management bargaining team did not establish goals or parameters because historically the Board accepts whatever the team recommends, as long as it is reasonable compared to other nearby similar type businesses. The Board has never been given their team parameters. This year the Company President, who is under fire from the Board, is playing it safe. The President has requested directed the team to set goals for the Board to review before the next session. He wants to be competitive with other similar nearby industries, but does not want to give away the farm.

** The company research department provided the team with the standards information. The Board wants to be competitive with other similar industries and has given the team permission to exceed the parameters within reason, if necessary, in order to get a settlement.

131

FINAL BLUEPRINT

Rated Issues	Goal	Settlement Standard	Final Settlement	Analysis +++, ++, +, 0,-, --
#1 Rated Issues 1.1				
1.2				
#2 Rated Issues 2.1				
2.2				
#3 Rated Issues 3.1				
3.2				

+++ meets goal, ++ meets settlement standard, + improvement, 0 little/no impact, ? questionable impact - minor loss, -- major loss

*This is an appropriate structure for a *small* package.

Counter No. _____

Date _____

Time _____

Counter No. _____

Date _____

Time _____

Counter No. _____

Date _____

Time _____

TENTATIVE AGREEMENT

_____   _____   _____
For the Union   Date   For Management

TENTATIVE AGREEMENT

_____   _____   _____
For the Union   Date   For Management

TENTATIVE AGREEMENT

_____ _____ _____
For the Union   Date   For Management

OBSERVATION FORM FOR SIMULATION EXERCISE

As you observe this bargaining simulation, make appropriate notes for both teams on the following skills, tactics, techniques, and strategies. Discuss your observations in the debrief following this simulation.

Bargaining Skills and Procedures	Association Team	Management Team
Team roles evident		
Team decision making process set and working		
Use of questioning skills		
Established goals and settlement standards		
Rated, ranked issues		
Utilized "no" as a response		
Had "flexibility" to bargain		
Worked off own proposal		
Met goals and settlement standards		

Notes:

_____

_____

_____

_____

TEAM DEBRIEF EXERCISE

1.   Some team members should switch places at table so people are seated differently and effectively end the role-playing.

2.   What was your team decision-making process? What way did you use to achieve this end?

3.   How did your team analyze or track the progress of the bargain?

4.   What were your team's goals and settlement standards?

5.   What were your team's settlement analysis results?

6.   How would you rate your settlement in relationship to your goals and settlement standards?

7.   Do you have any general comments about the simulation experience?

EPILOGUE

Bargaining is part art and part science, so be cognizant of opportunities and know when to settle on issues and/or packages, especially at closure. Developing a bargaining blueprint is the science part of the equation. The formula for successful bargaining is first knowing what to do, second knowing how to do it, and finally knowing when to do it. These are all a result of training, experience, and instincts.

When your head, heart, and gut are sending the same positive signals, then you probably be well served to follow your instincts. In the event your head, heart, or gut is sending negative signals, stop, reconsider and proceed with extreme caution.

Bon voyage on your bargaining journey!

Contact information:

Doc Dengenis

Bargaining Training and Strategy Consultant

503-803-4229

www.dengenisconsulting.com

docdengenis@gmail.com

9023 Mary Ave NW
#100
Seattle, WA 98117